ALPHABET FUN!

D1465318

SCHOLASTIC

Are you ready to have fun learning the alphabet with me?

Let's get started with awesome words that begin with the letter A!

Apple

Airplane

Blippi™

Astronaut

Ant

A

Arm

Avocado

Acorn

Alligator

3

Banana

Balloon

Ball

5

C

C words are so cool!

Car

Cloud

Cake

Carrot

Cup

Cat

E

E words are excellent!

Eagle

Eyeglasses

Ear

Exclamation point

Elephant

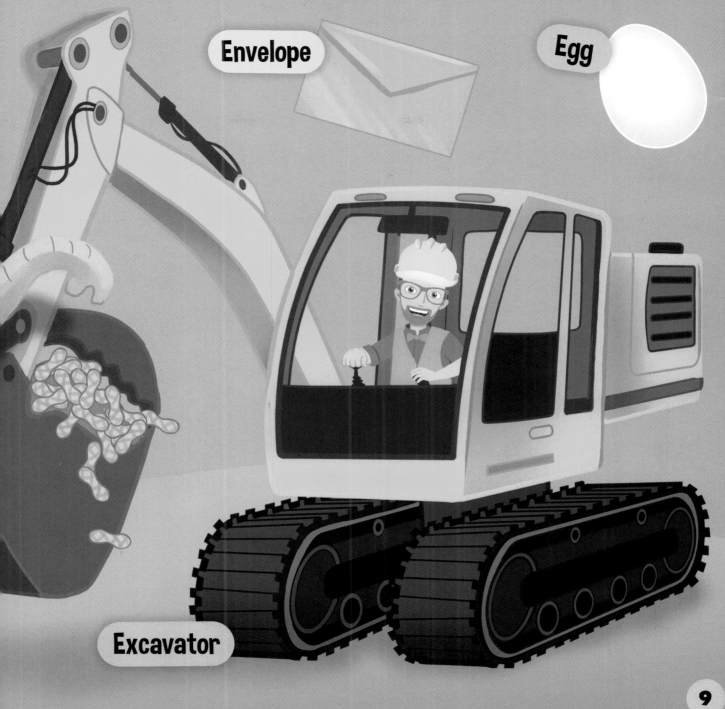

Envelope

Egg

Excavator

F

Words that begin with the letter F are fantastic!

Fox

Flower

Fork

Frog

Fence

Fire truck

10

G

G words are great!

Garbage truck

Gift

Gloves

Guitar

Gorilla

Grapes

11

I

I words are so interesting!

Ice-cream cone

Island

Ice-cream truck

Ice cubes

YUMMY ICE CREAM

Igloo

Iguana

13

J

Words that begin with the letter J make me want to jump for joy!

Jam jar

Juice

Jacket

Jump rope

Jeep

14

L

L words are so likeable!

Leaf

Lamp

Lemon

Lion

Lollipop

Ladder

M

My, my, there are so many marvellous M words!

Moon

Mouse

Mittens

Milk

Magnet

Monkey

Monster truck

N

Next up are some nice N words!

Nut

Nail

Necktie

Net

Notebook

Nest

O

Some outstanding words begin with an O!

Owl

Oven

Orange

Overalls

Olives

Octopus

19

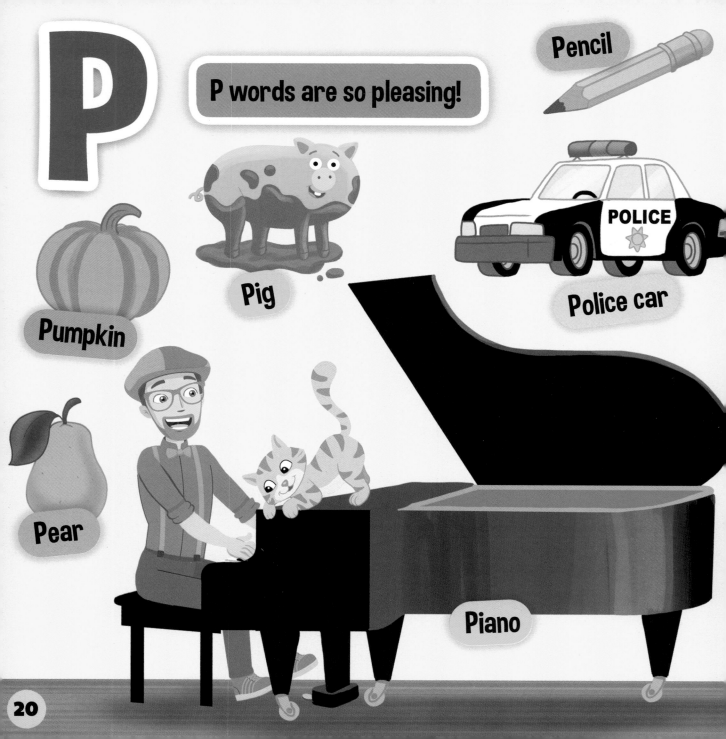

P

P words are so pleasing!

Pencil

Pig

Police car

Pumpkin

Pear

Piano

Q

Some quality words begin with a Q!

Queen

Question mark

?

Quilt

Quarter

Quartet

Quail

24

Tiger

Tail

Truck

Trolley

TAXI

Taxi

TAXI

Z

Let's zip through some Z words!

Zeppelin

Zucchini

Zebra

Zipper

ZZZZZ

Zigzag

Now you know all the letters of the alphabet! Which one is your favourite?

Blippi

A B C D E F G H I
J K L M N O P Q R
S T U V W X Y Z

For even more fun, listen to the audio CD that comes with this book and sing along with Blippi!